The Energy Reset

Simple Daily Steps to Beat Fatigue, (
Recharge Your Body and Mind — W(
Stay Energised All Day Long

CW01500259

Amelia Walsh

The Everyday Reset Series

This book is part of the *Everyday Reset* series: practical, uplifting guides designed to help you make small, sustainable changes that transform daily life. Each book focuses on one key area — gratitude, decluttering, walking, connection, energy — giving you simple tools to reset your habits, your mindset, and your wellbeing.

Praise for the Everyday Reset Approach

Readers love the *Everyday Reset* books for their:

- Warm, encouraging tone.

- Practical, realistic strategies.

- Focus on small steps that add up to big results.

- Balance of personal insight and science-backed advice.

Disclaimer

This book is written for informational and educational purposes only. It is not intended as medical advice, nor is it a substitute for professional care. Always consult a qualified healthcare provider before making changes to your diet, exercise, sleep, or health routines, particularly if you have any underlying health conditions or concerns.

The author has made every effort to ensure the accuracy of the information contained in this book, but the responsibility for your health choices rests with you.

Dedication

To everyone who has ever felt too tired to keep going —
may this book remind you that energy can be restored, one
small reset at a time.

CONTENTS

Introduction: From Running on Empty to Fully Alive

If you've picked up this book, there's a good chance you're tired. Not just the "I stayed up too late watching TV" kind of tired, but the deep weariness that seems to creep into every part of life. The kind of tiredness where coffee becomes a lifeline, where afternoons feel like uphill climbs, and where your mind struggles to stay clear and focused.

I know that feeling well.

For years, I juggled a full-time job, caring for a young child, and the chaos of two dogs who seemed to have limitless energy even when I didn't. Add in the emotional strain of a difficult break-up, and I often felt like I was running on empty — stretched so thin that even the smallest things became overwhelming. There were mornings when I woke up already exhausted, afternoons when I could barely think straight, and evenings when I crashed into bed too drained to do anything meaningful.

I kept telling myself it was just "life" — that being tired, stressed, and foggy was inevitable when you were busy, responsible, and holding everything together. But deep down, I knew it wasn't sustainable.

The turning point came when I realised that energy isn't something we either have or don't have — it's something we can nurture, reset, and rebuild. Not through dramatic overhauls or impossible routines, but through small, practical shifts in how we eat, move, think, and recover.

That's why I wrote *The Energy Reset*.

This book isn't about perfection. You won't find complicated health plans, rigid diets, or impossible

1

morning routines here. Instead, you'll find simple, everyday resets that fit into a busy life — the kind of small changes that add up, quietly but powerfully, to make you feel clearer, lighter, and more alive.

And because I know how overwhelming change can feel when you're already tired, this book is designed to take you step by step. Each chapter tackles one area of your energy — the hidden drains, the daily habits, and the simple resets that can make all the difference.

Here's a quick overview of what you'll discover:

- In **Chapter 1**, we'll look at why you're always tired and why quick fixes never last.

- **Chapter 2** reveals the "energy equation" — how sleep, food, movement, and mindset all interact.

- In **Chapters 3 and 4**, you'll learn how to start your mornings with strength by using light, movement, and mindset as natural energisers.

- **Chapters 5 and 6** focus on how to fuel without the crash and beat the dreaded midday slump with quick, practical resets.

- In **Chapter 7**, we'll explore why movement should energise, not exhaust you — and how to make it work in your real life.

- **Chapters 8 and 9** show you how to manage stress and shift from "always tired" thinking into an energised mindset.

- Finally, **Chapter 10** brings it all together with a 30-day Energy Reset plan to help you build lasting energy habits that stick.

My hope is that by the end of this journey, you'll not only understand what drains your energy but also have a realistic toolkit to recharge it — without turning your whole life upside down.

Because you don't need to keep running on empty. You can reset your energy. You can feel refreshed, focused, and motivated again. And you can do it one small, simple step at a time.

So if you've been living on autopilot — tired, stressed, and barely holding it together — this is your invitation to pause, reset, and take back control of your energy. You don't need more willpower, more coffee, or more hours in the day. You simply need the right habits, built one small step at a time.

Every page of this book is here to guide you back to feeling clear, strong, and fully alive.

Your reset starts now.

Let's begin.

Chapter 1: Why You're Always Tired

If there's one phrase I've heard — and said — more than almost anything else, it's this: *"I'm tired."*

It slips out in conversation, almost unconsciously, when someone asks how you are. It runs through your mind in the morning when the alarm goes off. It's the undercurrent of your day, the thing you feel in your body before you've even had the chance to think about it.

But here's the truth: while feeling tired is common, it's not normal. At least, not in the way many of us accept it to be.

The problem is, tiredness has become so universal that we treat it like the weather — just part of life, unavoidable, out of our control. And yet when you really pause and look at it, much of what makes us exhausted isn't inevitable. It's the result of habits, routines, and pressures that quietly chip away at our energy until running on empty feels like the default.

In this chapter, I want to help you understand *why* you're always tired. Not just in vague terms, but in clear, practical ways that make sense. Because once you know the hidden drains on your energy, you can start to do something about them.

The Myth of "Just Busy"

When I was working full-time, raising a young child, and managing the daily chaos of two dogs, my default explanation for exhaustion was simple: *"I'm just busy."*

And yes, life was full. But being busy is not the same thing as being drained. There's a kind of tiredness that comes from a long, meaningful day that still feels satisfying — and then there's the bone-deep exhaustion that leaves you foggy, irritable, and empty.

The truth is, busyness was only part of the story. What really kept me stuck in fatigue was the way I managed (or didn't manage) the basics: sleep, food, movement, and stress. And once I started to make small resets in each of those areas, the difference was remarkable.

Energy Leaks: The Hidden Drains

Think of your energy like a phone battery. Every morning, you wake up with a certain charge. The way you eat, move, think, and live either helps you *hold on to that charge* — or drains it faster than you can replenish it.

Here are some of the most common energy leaks:

1. **Poor Sleep Quality**
   You might be in bed for eight hours, but if your sleep is light, broken, or restless, you'll wake up unrefreshed. Many people underestimate how much poor sleep contributes to their daytime fatigue.

2. **Sugar & Caffeine Rollercoasters**
   That morning coffee or mid-afternoon chocolate bar gives a short burst of energy — but often followed by a crash that leaves you more tired than before. Over time, your body becomes reliant on these spikes just to function.

3. **Sedentary Habits**
   It sounds counterintuitive, but sitting still for long stretches actually *drains* energy. Movement circulates oxygen, stimulates your muscles, and wakes up your brain.

4. **Chronic Stress**
   Stress is like a background app running on your phone — constantly draining the battery, even when you think you're resting. Worry, tension, and constant pressure keep your body in "alert mode," leaving you depleted.

5. **Mental Overload**
   Decision fatigue, information overload, and endless to-do lists all weigh heavily on your brain. A foggy mind is one of the clearest signs of low energy.

6. **Emotional Strain**
   Going through challenges — like a break-up, grief, or ongoing conflict — can sap your energy in ways that physical tiredness alone doesn't explain. Emotional health and energy are closely linked.

The Quick Fix Trap

When we're drained, our instinct is to reach for something that promises instant relief: caffeine, sugar, scrolling, or even just collapsing on the sofa. And in the moment, it works — a shot of energy, a moment of distraction, a little lift.

But these quick fixes come with a cost. Coffee late in the day disrupts your sleep, sugar spikes your blood sugar then leaves you crashing, and too much passive screen time can leave you feeling more drained than restored.

The problem isn't that these things are "bad" — it's that they don't *restore* energy. They borrow it from tomorrow. And when you're already running on empty, that's a cycle you can't afford.

The Real Causes of Fatigue

So if it's not just busyness, and not just a lack of willpower, what's really behind constant tiredness? Here are the five main categories you'll see repeated throughout this book:

1. **Sleep** – Not just quantity, but quality. Deep, restorative rest is essential for energy.

2. **Nutrition** – What you eat and drink directly affects your energy levels hour by hour.

3. **Movement** – The right kind of activity boosts energy, while too much or too little can deplete it.

4. **Stress** – Chronic tension drains both body and mind, leaving you running on fumes.

5. **Mindset** – How you *think* about energy shapes your behaviour, your habits, and even your biology.

My Breaking Point

I remember one particular day when everything hit me at once. I'd had a rough night's sleep after staying up too late answering emails. My child woke early, the dogs needed walking, and I was already on edge before the day had even begun.

By mid-morning, I'd had two coffees and was still yawning through meetings. My head felt foggy, my patience was thin, and by the afternoon I found myself staring blankly at the computer screen, unable to string a clear thought together.

That night, as I collapsed into bed, I thought: *Is this it? Is this just what adult life feels like now?*

It was that moment of honesty that made me start looking for a different way. Not a total life overhaul, not an unrealistic wellness plan, but small resets I could actually do.

And that's what this book is about.

The Good News

Here's the part I want you to take to heart: your tiredness is not inevitable. Feeling drained all the time is not your natural state.

With the right adjustments — even small ones — you can reclaim steady, reliable energy. You can wake up feeling refreshed, keep your focus through the day, and still have something left in the tank for the things that matter most.

The rest of this book will show you how.

Looking Ahead

In the chapters that follow, we'll build a complete picture of what really fuels your energy — and how to reset it, one simple step at a time:

- In **Chapter 2**, you'll discover the "energy equation" — how sleep, food, movement, and mindset all connect.

- **Chapters 3 and 4** will show you how to start your mornings strong, with light, movement, and mindset as natural energisers.

- In **Chapters 5 and 6**, we'll explore how to fuel without the crash and beat the midday slump with quick resets.

- **Chapter 7** will help you rethink movement so it energises, not exhausts you.

- **Chapters 8 and 9** focus on stress and mindset —
  the hidden energy thieves we can learn to manage.

- And finally, **Chapter 10** brings it all together with
  a 30-day Energy Reset plan to help you embed
  these changes into lasting habits.

Reflect & Reset

Take a moment to pause and reflect:

- When do you feel most drained during the day?

- What "quick fixes" do you usually reach for when
  you're tired?

- Do you think your tiredness is more physical,
  mental, or emotional right now?

Jot down a few thoughts. This will help you notice your
personal "energy leaks" — and give you a starting point for
the resets to come.

Chapter 2: The Energy Equation

If you want to change anything in your life, it helps to understand how it works first. Energy is no different. It might feel mysterious or out of your control, but in reality, your daily energy is the result of a handful of key factors working together.

I like to think of it as an equation. Not in a complicated, mathematical way — but as a simple formula you can use to understand what fuels you and what drains you. Once you see how the pieces fit, you'll know exactly where to make small changes that deliver big results.

Energy Isn't Just Physical

Most people think of energy in purely physical terms: how awake you feel, how heavy your body feels, or how much stamina you have. But energy is more than that.

Energy has at least four dimensions:

1. **Physical energy** – How your body feels and functions.

2. **Mental energy** – How sharp, focused, and clear your thinking is.

3. **Emotional energy** – How balanced, positive, and resilient you feel.

4. **Social energy** – How much connection, interaction, and support you have from others.

All four feed into each other. For example, poor sleep (physical) clouds your thinking (mental), which makes you snappier with loved ones (emotional), which can affect your relationships (social). On the flip side, a good night's rest can sharpen your mind, lift your mood, and make you more present with others.

This is why the energy equation is so powerful: once you strengthen one area, the benefits ripple outwards.

The Core Elements of the Energy Equation

So, what makes up your personal energy equation? At its simplest, there are five main components.

1. Sleep

Think of sleep as your nightly recharge. Without it, nothing else works properly. It restores your body, clears toxins from your brain, consolidates memory, and balances your hormones. Poor sleep is one of the biggest contributors to fatigue, brain fog, and low mood.

2. Nutrition

Food is fuel, but not all fuel is equal. The quality, timing, and balance of what you eat determines whether your energy is steady or unstable. Sugary snacks or heavy meals can drain you, while balanced, nutrient-rich food keeps your energy consistent.

3. Movement

Movement isn't just about burning calories — it's about circulation, oxygenation, and activating your muscles and mind. The right kind of movement gives you more energy, not less. Too much intensity, or too little activity, and your body feels sluggish.

4. Stress Management

Stress is an energy thief. It keeps your body in a constant state of alert, which uses up resources faster than you can replenish them. Managing stress doesn't mean eliminating it (that's impossible), but learning how to downshift from high alert back to calm.

5. Mindset

Perhaps the most underestimated factor. If you constantly tell yourself "I'm always tired," your brain believes it and shapes your behaviour to match. Shifting your mindset doesn't mean ignoring reality — it means choosing thoughts that help you recharge instead of reinforcing fatigue.

The Balance of Inputs and Outputs

Here's the simplest way to think about the energy equation:

Energy Inputs – Energy Outputs = Daily Energy Balance

Inputs are the things that give you energy: sleep, nourishing food, movement, rest, positive emotions, connection, purpose.

Outputs are the things that drain you: work demands, family responsibilities, stress, lack of rest, poor diet, negative emotions, information overload.

When your inputs outweigh your outputs, you feel energised. When outputs exceed inputs, you feel tired, drained, and depleted.

The challenge is that many people are constantly running in deficit — giving out more energy than they put back in. That's when fatigue becomes the default.

Why Willpower Isn't the Answer

You might be thinking: "I know I should eat better, sleep more, and exercise... but I just don't have the willpower."

But willpower isn't the problem. Energy is.

When you're depleted, your brain craves easy fixes: caffeine, sugar, scrolling, skipping exercise. That doesn't mean you're weak — it means your system is trying to conserve energy. The solution isn't to push harder with discipline, but to reset the underlying inputs and outputs so your energy naturally rises.

When you restore your energy balance, motivation follows. You don't need to force yourself to do what's good for you — it starts to feel easier, even appealing.

The Compounding Effect of Small Changes

The beauty of the energy equation is that even tiny adjustments can make a noticeable difference. Go to bed 30 minutes earlier, and your sleep input increases. Swap one sugary snack for a protein-rich one, and your nutrition input strengthens. Take a five-minute walk at lunchtime, and your movement input grows.

Each small shift adds to your input side, gradually tipping the balance back in your favour. Over time, those small deposits compound, like interest in a bank account.

Personal Reflection: My Own Energy Equation

During the hardest season of my life — balancing full-time work, parenting, two dogs, and the emotional weight of a break-up — I felt like I had no margin. I thought I had to keep pushing through, sacrificing sleep, skipping meals, and relying on caffeine to get by.

Looking back, I can see my equation clearly: far too many outputs, not enough inputs. I was draining my energy faster than I could restore it.

The first time I flipped the balance was when I started prioritising just one thing: sleep. I committed to a consistent bedtime, even when work was unfinished or chores were waiting. Within a week, my mornings felt lighter. That small change encouraged me to add another input — short walks. Then another — more balanced meals. Step by step, the equation shifted.

That's when I realised energy isn't a mystery. It's math. If you keep withdrawing without depositing, you'll go into the red. But if you start topping up your inputs, even in small ways, you can get back into the black.

Looking Ahead

The rest of this book is designed to help you strengthen each part of your energy equation. Here's how the chapters fit together:

- **Chapters 3 and 4** will show you how to start your mornings strong by using light, movement, and mindset as natural energisers.

- **Chapters 5 and 6** will guide you to fuel your body without the crash and tackle the dreaded midday slump.

- **Chapter 7** will reframe exercise so it becomes a source of energy, not exhaustion.

- **Chapters 8 and 9** will help you manage stress and reshape your mindset — two of the most overlooked but powerful parts of the equation.

- Finally, **Chapter 10** will give you a 30-day Energy Reset plan to put it all together in a way that's realistic and sustainable.

Reflect & Reset

Take a moment to think about your own energy equation.

- What inputs (sleep, food, movement, rest, connection) are you currently neglecting?

- What outputs (work, stress, responsibilities, habits) are draining you the most?

- If you had to improve just one input this week, what would it be?

Write it down. This reflection isn't about judgment — it's about awareness. Once you see where the leaks are, you can begin to patch them and start tipping the balance back in your favour.

Chapter 3: Start Strong: Waking Up with Energy

Mornings set the tone for the entire day. Think about the difference between the days you wake up refreshed and the days you wake up groggy. When you start well, everything feels lighter. You're more focused, more patient, and more able to deal with what comes your way. When you start poorly, even small tasks feel like uphill battles.

For many people, mornings feel more like survival than opportunity. The alarm goes off, you hit snooze once (or three times), drag yourself out of bed, and immediately reach for coffee. If you have children, pets, or work emails demanding your attention, you might not even have those few quiet minutes for yourself. By the time you're out the door or at your desk, you already feel behind.

But what if mornings could feel different? What if you could start your day with more energy, clarity, and calm — without needing an extra hour or complicated routine? That's what this chapter is about: creating a realistic, energising start that works in the context of a busy life.

Why Mornings Matter

Your body and brain operate on a circadian rhythm — an internal 24-hour clock that regulates energy, mood, digestion, and more. The first hour after waking acts like a reset button. What you do in those early minutes sends signals to your body about what kind of day it's going to be.

If you scroll on your phone, rush, or immediately reach for caffeine, your body receives stress signals—setting you up for fatigue and fog later on. But if you start with daylight, movement, and calm, your body receives wake-up signals that naturally boost alertness, regulate hormones, and increase energy.

The Three Morning Energy Switches

There are three simple switches you can flip each morning to set the tone right:

1. Light – A few minutes of natural light each morning resets your internal clock.

2. Movement – Simple activity gets oxygen flowing and shakes off sleep inertia.

3. Mindset – Setting a small, positive intention first thing lightly guides your emotion and focus.

Make Your Bed: A Tiny Act That Matters

A practice often attributed to Admiral William H. McRaven illustrates the ripple effect of small actions. In his famous commencement speech at the University of Texas, he shared a memory from his Navy SEAL training:

Every morning, the instructors would inspect the trainees' beds with military precision—corners square, covers tight, pillow perfectly centered. Making your bed was one of the very first tasks of the day. McRaven explained that completing this simple task instilled pride and set a momentum for the day:

"If you make your bed every morning you will have accomplished the first task of the day. It will give you a small sense of pride, and it will encourage you to do another task and another and another... And if by chance you have a miserable day, you will come home to a bed that is made — that you made — and a made bed gives you encouragement that tomorrow will be better."

— Admiral William H. McRaven

This simple, practical action underscores a core idea of this chapter: **beginning the day with one deliberate, meaningful reset creates a ripple effect of intention, clarity, and momentum**. That's why the rituals I'm encouraging here are not complex—they're powerful because they're small, real-life achievable, and profoundly effective.

Step One: Rethink the Alarm

How you wake up matters. A jarring alarm can feel like being pushed into the day. If possible, use an alarm that wakes you gently, whether by light or a gradually rising sound. Crucially, place your alarm out of easy reach. Hitting snooze delivers fragmented, low-quality sleep rather than rest. A single alarm prompts movement and activates your will right away.

Step Two: Light Before Screens

Skip the screen time first. Your body craves natural light to align cortisol and melatonin levels. Even a brief burst of daylight—just open the curtains or step outside—anchors your body's rhythm and grants a subtle mood and energy lift.

Step Three: Gentle Movement

No need for intense morning workouts. Choose movement that lightly activates your body:

- A short walk

- Calming stretching

- A couple of yoga poses

Even two minutes can boost circulation, oxygenate your brain, and raise alertness gently—without draining your energy reserves.

Step Four: Hydrate Before Caffeine

Your body wakes slightly dehydrated. Drinking water right away helps with circulation, clarity, and focus. Coffee can wait—enjoy it later alongside a healthy breakfast so it becomes a complement, not a crutch.

Step Five: A Mindset Cue

Mindset in the first moments of the day holds surprising power. Avoid starting on autopilot with "I'm so tired." Instead, nudge yourself gently: ask, "What am I looking forward to today?" This isn't forced positivity—it's a redirect toward calm anticipation, however small.

Building a Morning Reset Ritual

Here's one example you can try. It takes less than ten minutes:

1. Wake with a single alarm, placed away from you.
2. Drink a glass of water.
3. Open curtains or step outside briefly.
4. Move gently (stretch, walk, rotate).
5. Pause to think of one thing you're gently looking forward to.

That's all. Simple changes. Minimal time. Powerful effects.

Personal Reflection: When Mornings Felt Impossible

Balancing a full-time job, a young child, and two energetic dogs, mornings often felt chaotic. I used to believe I'd never have space for calm or routine. But once I shifted my mindset—aiming for tiny wins rather than perfection—I started my days better. Just water before coffee, daylight while the kettle boiled, and one minute of stretch became daily resets that began to shift my energy for the better.

Why Small Shifts Matter

Small actions are deceptively powerful. Remember the energy equation from Chapter 2: each input counts. One glass of water, a minute of light exposure, a gentle stretch— all add to your energy reserves. And because mornings influence the hours that follow, these tiny resets help shape the trajectory of your whole day.

Looking Ahead

In the next chapter, we unpack the three morning energy switches—light, movement, and mindset—in more detail. I'll guide you through adaptable ways to make them work, whether you have ten minutes or just two. For now, try one reset tomorrow morning—be intentional, be gentle, and notice how your day shifts.

Reflect & Reset

Take a moment:

- How do you usually begin your mornings?
- Which parts feel draining, and which feel energising?
- What's one small reset you could commit to tomorrow?

Write it down on a post-it, put it by your bed, or tape it to the kettle. The next time you wake up, that note will remind you: you can start your day with energy.

Chapter 4: Light, Movement, and Mindset

In the last chapter, we explored how mornings set the tone for the entire day and how even the smallest actions—like drinking water or opening the curtains—can change the trajectory of your energy. Now it's time to look more closely at the three most powerful switches you can flip each morning: light, movement, and mindset.

These three elements may seem almost too simple. But that's their strength. They are rooted in biology, psychology, and daily rhythm. They don't require extra time, equipment, or money. They're always available, and they work together to wake you up in a way that feels natural and sustainable.

The First Switch: Light

Light is one of the strongest signals your body has for waking up. When natural light enters your eyes in the morning, it tells your brain that it's daytime. Your brain then reduces melatonin (the sleep hormone) and increases cortisol (a hormone that helps you feel alert). This process resets your circadian rhythm and anchors your body clock for the day.

If you've ever struggled with grogginess even after eight hours of sleep, lack of morning light may be part of the reason. Many of us wake in dim rooms, go straight into artificial lighting, and then spend the day indoors. Our bodies miss out on the vital cue that comes from daylight.

Practical Resets with Light

- **Step outside for five minutes** as soon as you can. Even cloudy skies provide more natural light than indoor bulbs.

- **Open your curtains fully** and position yourself near a window while you eat breakfast or get ready.

- **If mornings are dark where you live**, consider a light therapy lamp. These mimic daylight and can help your body clock stay on track, especially in winter months.

Light exposure early in the day doesn't just help mornings—it improves your sleep at night. By resetting your body clock, you make it easier to fall asleep in the evening, which in turn creates a virtuous cycle of better mornings.

The Second Switch: Movement

The second switch is movement. After hours of being still in bed, your circulation and oxygen flow are sluggish. Even a small amount of activity increases blood flow, delivers oxygen to your brain, and shakes off the heaviness of sleep inertia.

This doesn't need to be formal exercise. In fact, overly intense workouts first thing can sometimes make you more tired later in the day. The goal is to "switch on" your body, not to exhaust it.

Practical Resets with Movement

- **Stretch while the kettle boils.** Simple arm reaches, torso twists, or a forward fold can loosen stiffness and increase circulation.

- **Take a brisk walk.** If you have a dog, their morning walk is a built-in reset. If not, even two minutes of walking outside helps.

- **Try a micro-routine.** Ten squats, ten wall push-ups, ten calf raises. Less than three minutes, but enough to activate your muscles.

- **Use stairs instead of lifts or escalators.** If you commute, the first movement you choose sets a precedent for the day.

Remember: movement doesn't need to be perfect to be effective. The key is consistency. Gentle, repeated activation each morning signals to your body that it's time to be awake, energised, and ready.

The Third Switch: Mindset

The third switch is mindset, and it's often the most overlooked. What you focus on in the first hour of the day has a disproportionate influence on your energy. If you begin with thoughts like "I'm exhausted" or "I can't face this," you set your brain into a negative scanning mode—it starts to look for proof of those beliefs all day.

But if you begin with a small, intentional thought, you nudge your mind towards clarity and positivity. This isn't about forced affirmations or pretending life is perfect. It's about giving yourself a gentle direction for your thoughts before the day sweeps you away.

Practical Resets with Mindset

- **Ask one question:** "What's one thing I'm looking forward to today?" It doesn't have to be big. A coffee with a friend, a walk at lunch, or a favourite TV show can be enough.

- **Gratitude note.** Write down one thing you're grateful for. This shifts your brain from scarcity to abundance, opening up energy for the day.

- **Set a micro-intention.** Instead of vague goals like "be productive," choose something small: "I'll finish one important task before lunch."

When you deliberately choose your first thought, you stop your brain from defaulting to stress, worry, or fatigue. That one small choice can echo through your mood, focus, and energy all day.

How the Switches Work Together

Each of these switches—light, movement, and mindset—is powerful on its own. But the real magic comes when you combine them. Imagine this sequence:

- You step outside for five minutes of daylight.

- While outside, you stretch your arms or take a short walk.

- While moving, you ask yourself, "What's one thing I'm looking forward to today?"

In less than ten minutes, you've activated your body clock, boosted circulation, and given your mind a positive direction. That combination is far more effective than any one of them alone.

And the best part? You don't need a perfect morning to make it work. Even if children, pets, or work demands start pulling you in different directions, slipping in just one of these switches will make a noticeable difference.

Personal Reflection: Finding My Own Morning Switches

For a long time, my mornings felt chaotic. Between getting my child ready, walking the dogs, and rushing to work, I felt like the day was controlling me before I had a chance to catch up.

What helped was realising I didn't need a full hour-long morning routine. I simply needed to find a few switches I could reliably flip. For me, it started with drinking water and opening the curtains wide while I made breakfast. Later, I added a short stretch and the practice of naming one thing I was looking forward to.

Those small steps didn't magically fix everything, but they shifted my mornings from frantic to grounded. And that shift carried through into the rest of the day.

Why This Works

The science behind these switches is clear. Light resets your circadian rhythm. Movement increases circulation and oxygen. Mindset shapes the lens through which you interpret the day. None of them take much time, but together, they transform the way you start.

Remember the story from the last chapter about Admiral McRaven and making your bed? These switches work in the same way. They're not grand gestures—they're small wins that set a tone of clarity, focus, and control. And once you've begun with intention, it's easier to keep that momentum going.

Looking Ahead

In the next two chapters, we'll move from mornings into the rest of your day. We'll look at how to fuel your body without the crashes that come from sugar and caffeine, and how to beat the dreaded midday slump with quick resets you can do in minutes.

But for now, your focus is simple: choose one switch—light, movement, or mindset—to try tomorrow. Start with what feels easiest, and build from there. You don't need all three at once. Remember, energy is about consistency, not perfection.

Reflect & Reset

Pause and consider:

- Which of the three switches do you already use, even unintentionally?

- Which one feels most realistic for you to add tomorrow?

- How could you combine two or more into a short, personal ritual?

Jot down your plan. Keep it visible where you'll see it first thing in the morning. Tomorrow, when you wake, remind yourself: energy isn't something you wait for. It's something you can switch on.

Chapter 5: Fuel Without the Crash

If energy were as simple as "calories in, calories out," most of us wouldn't struggle. We'd eat, we'd be fuelled, and that would be the end of it. But as you already know, food isn't just fuel — it's information. Every bite you take sends signals to your body that either stabilise your energy or send it on a rollercoaster of spikes and crashes.

Think about your last midday slump. Maybe it hit around 3 p.m. You felt foggy, heavy, and tempted by biscuits, chocolate, or another coffee. You gave in, and for a short time you felt better. But an hour later, you were back where you started, only more drained. That's the cycle of energy crashes.

The good news? It's not inevitable. With a few small shifts, you can eat and drink in ways that give you steady, reliable energy — without cutting out entire food groups or living on salads and green smoothies. This chapter will show you how.

Why Food Matters for Energy

Food is your body's main source of energy, but it works in more complex ways than just "fuel." Different foods are digested at different speeds, affect blood sugar differently, and trigger different hormonal responses.

When you eat sugary or refined foods, your blood sugar spikes quickly. Your body responds by releasing insulin, which brings your blood sugar down — sometimes too far. That "crash" is what leaves you tired, foggy, and craving more sugar. Over time, this rollercoaster pattern keeps you in a cycle of highs and lows, instead of steady energy.

Balanced meals, on the other hand, release energy more slowly and steadily. They keep your blood sugar stable, which means fewer spikes, fewer crashes, and a more consistent level of energy throughout the day.

The Big Three: Protein, Fibre, and Healthy Fats

If you want to avoid crashes, these three are your allies:

1. **Protein**
   Protein takes longer to digest than simple carbohydrates, so it slows down the release of energy. It also supports muscles, hormones, and overall repair.

   o Examples: eggs, yoghurt, chicken, fish, beans, lentils, nuts, seeds.

2. **Fibre**
   Fibre also slows digestion and helps keep blood sugar stable. It's found in fruits, vegetables, whole grains, beans, and legumes.

   o Think of fibre as the "steadying hand" that keeps your energy even.

3. **Healthy Fats**
   Fats take the longest to digest, meaning they give a slow, steady release of energy. They also help you feel satisfied and prevent overeating later.

   o Examples: olive oil, avocado, nuts, seeds, oily fish.

When your meals and snacks include a mix of these three, your energy levels stay more balanced.

The Problem with Quick Fixes

It's tempting to rely on things that give fast relief. Coffee perks you up, biscuits give a sugar rush, and energy drinks promise instant focus. But they all work the same way: short bursts, followed by inevitable crashes.

That doesn't mean you can never have them. Coffee can be enjoyable and even beneficial when timed well. Treats can be part of a balanced diet. The key is not to *depend* on them as your main energy sources. Otherwise, your day becomes a cycle of highs and lows, never quite finding steady ground.

Breakfast: Your First Fuel of the Day

The first meal you eat plays a huge role in how your energy unfolds. Many people skip breakfast, grab something sugary on the go, or rely on caffeine to carry them through. But this sets you up for rollercoasters later.

A better approach is to think of breakfast as your first chance to stabilise blood sugar. Aim for protein, fibre, and healthy fats together.

Examples:

- Scrambled eggs on wholegrain toast with avocado.

- Yoghurt with berries, chia seeds, and a handful of nuts.

- Overnight oats with milk, flaxseeds, and nut butter.

If mornings are rushed, even something as simple as a boiled egg and a banana is better than a pastry and coffee.

Lunch: The Midday Anchor

Lunch is where many people lose energy. A heavy meal can make you sluggish, while a light meal of just salad or bread can leave you hungry and drained. The key is balance.

Examples:

- A wrap with chicken, hummus, and mixed vegetables.
- Lentil soup with wholegrain bread.
- Salmon with quinoa and roasted vegetables.

Adding vegetables boosts fibre, adding protein keeps you steady, and healthy fats help you stay satisfied until dinner.

Snacks: Smart Refuelling

Snacking often gets a bad reputation, but it's not the act of snacking that causes problems — it's the type of snack. A biscuit gives you a short-lived lift. A balanced snack supports you until your next meal.

Smart snack examples:

- Apple slices with peanut butter.
- A small handful of nuts with a piece of fruit.
- Greek yoghurt with chia seeds.
- Wholegrain crackers with cheese or hummus.

The trick is to combine a carbohydrate (fruit, cracker) with protein or fat (nuts, cheese, yoghurt) so the energy release is steady.

Hydration: The Forgotten Energy Source

Dehydration is one of the most overlooked causes of fatigue. Even mild dehydration — as little as one or two percent of body weight — can make you feel tired, foggy, and unmotivated.

Aim to drink water steadily throughout the day, not just in big gulps when you're already thirsty. Herbal teas and sparkling water also count. If you're a coffee drinker, balance each cup with a glass of water to avoid dehydration.

Caffeine: Friend or Foe?

Caffeine isn't the enemy, but timing is everything. A coffee at the right time can give you focus. Too much, or too late in the day, and it can disrupt your sleep, which drains your energy in the long run.

Tips for using caffeine wisely:

- Wait at least an hour after waking before your first coffee. This allows your body's natural cortisol to peak, rather than masking it.

- Avoid caffeine after 2 p.m. so it doesn't interfere with your sleep cycle.

- Stick to one or two cups, and avoid turning it into a constant drip feed.

When used strategically, caffeine can be a helpful ally. When overused, it becomes a crutch that undermines the very energy you're trying to restore.

Personal Reflection: My Own Crashes

During one particularly stressful season, my daily routine looked like this: skip breakfast, grab a coffee on the way to work, and raid the vending machine around 3 p.m. By dinner, I was ravenous and ate whatever was easiest. Unsurprisingly, my energy was all over the place.

The first reset I made was adding a protein-based breakfast. Suddenly, the mid-morning slump disappeared. Then I started bringing balanced snacks with me, so I wasn't at the mercy of the vending machine. Over time, these small adjustments transformed my afternoons from foggy to focused.

It wasn't about being perfect — it was about being intentional with the fuel I gave my body.

Looking Ahead

In the next chapter, we'll look at what happens when energy dips anyway — the dreaded midday slump — and how to reset in minutes. Because even with the best fuel, life happens, and knowing how to recharge quickly is an essential skill.

Reflect & Reset

Take a moment to consider your own eating patterns.

- Do you often skip meals, then crash later?

- Which snacks or drinks give you quick highs but leave you drained?

- Where could you add more protein, fibre, or healthy fats to steady your energy?

Write down one simple adjustment you could try tomorrow — whether it's eating breakfast, swapping your snack, or drinking more water.

Chapter 6: Beat the Midday Slump

It's the middle of the afternoon. You've eaten lunch, your inbox is full, and your body feels like it's shutting down. Your eyelids are heavy, your brain is foggy, and you'd give almost anything for a nap. Sound familiar?

The midday slump is one of the most common energy struggles people face. Even when you've eaten well and slept enough, that dip between about 2 and 4 p.m. can feel unavoidable. The truth is, there are biological reasons behind it — but there are also simple ways to manage it so it doesn't derail your day.

Why the Slump Happens

Your body naturally runs in cycles of energy and alertness called ultradian rhythms. Roughly every 90 to 120 minutes, your energy rises and falls. By the afternoon, especially after eating lunch, those natural rhythms combine with digestion to create a dip.

Other factors can make it worse:

- **Heavy lunches** rich in refined carbs can trigger blood sugar crashes.

- **Dehydration** builds up gradually and peaks in the afternoon.

- **Lack of movement** after sitting for hours slows circulation and reduces alertness.

- **Mental fatigue** from focusing for too long without breaks depletes your brain's resources.

The key isn't to fight biology with more caffeine or sugar, but to work with your body's rhythm and use resets that restore energy in minutes.

Reset 1: Move Your Body

Movement is one of the fastest and most reliable ways to overcome the slump. Even a short burst gets blood flowing, oxygen circulating, and your brain re-engaged.

Ideas for quick movement resets:

- Stand up and walk around the room or down a hallway for 3–5 minutes.

- Do a few stretches at your desk: shoulder rolls, neck stretches, standing side bends.

- Take the stairs instead of the lift.

- If you work from home, step outside for a short walk.

It doesn't need to be a workout. Think of it as pressing the "reset" button on your body and mind.

Reset 2: Change Your Visual Focus

Staring at a screen for hours is draining. Your eyes get tired, your posture slumps, and your brain zones out. Simply changing what you're looking at can recharge you.

- Try the **20-20-20 rule**: every 20 minutes, look at something 20 feet away for 20 seconds.

- Step outside and look at the horizon or the sky for a few minutes.

- If that's not possible, even gazing out of a window helps reset your focus.

This small shift gives your brain and eyes a break, refreshing your concentration.

Reset 3: Hydrate

Many afternoon slumps are really dehydration in disguise. By the time you feel thirsty, you're already behind. A glass of water, herbal tea, or sparkling water can perk you up in ways that rival coffee.

Make it easy: keep a water bottle at your desk or in your bag and sip regularly throughout the day. If plain water feels boring, add slices of lemon, cucumber, or mint for variety.

Reset 4: Use Caffeine Strategically

Caffeine can help — but timing and dosage matter. A small cup of coffee or green tea early in the afternoon can give you focus without interfering with your evening sleep. Too much, too late, and it disrupts your sleep cycle, which leaves you more tired tomorrow.

If you're sensitive to caffeine, try switching to green tea, which contains less caffeine and the amino acid L-theanine, known for promoting calm alertness.

Reset 5: Breathe and Reset Your Mind

Stress and overwhelm can amplify the slump. A simple breathing exercise can reduce stress and restore energy quickly.

Try this:

- Inhale through your nose for a count of four.

- Hold for a count of four.

- Exhale through your mouth for a count of six.

- Repeat for two or three minutes.

This lowers stress hormones, increases oxygen intake, and leaves you calmer and more alert.

Reset 6: Eat a Smart Snack

If your slump is hunger-related, a balanced snack can help — but choose carefully. Sugary treats will spike your energy and crash it again. Instead, aim for a mix of protein and slow-release carbs.

Smart snack ideas:

- An apple with almond butter.

- A small pot of yoghurt with seeds or nuts.

- Carrot sticks with hummus.

- Wholegrain crackers with cheese.

These give you a steady lift without the rollercoaster.

Reset 7: Break the Mental Pattern

Sometimes the slump isn't physical at all — it's mental fatigue from doing the same thing for too long. Changing tasks or shifting focus for a short time can restore energy.

- Switch from analytical tasks to creative ones (or vice versa).

- Tidy your desk for five minutes.

- Write a quick to-do list for tomorrow.

- Read something light that shifts your mindset.

A short change of pace can free up mental bandwidth and make the rest of the day more productive.

The Myth of Powering Through

Many of us believe the answer to the slump is to simply push harder. More coffee, more focus, more grit. But working against your body's rhythms only makes fatigue worse.

By allowing yourself short resets, you actually gain time because you restore the energy needed to finish tasks more effectively. Taking five minutes to reset can save you hours of sluggish, unproductive effort.

Personal Reflection: My Midday Struggles

For a long time, my afternoons were my weakest point. After lunch, I'd reach automatically for another coffee or something sweet. It gave me a temporary lift, but within an hour I was yawning again, staring blankly at the screen.

What changed was adding short walks into my day. At first it felt indulgent — surely I didn't have time to leave my desk. But I noticed I returned sharper and could finish work faster. Later, I added small snacks like nuts or fruit instead of chocolate. Those simple changes made afternoons feel manageable instead of miserable.

Looking Ahead

Now that we've tackled mornings, fuelling, and the midday slump, we're ready to turn to movement in a broader sense. In the next chapter, we'll explore why the right kind of movement can give you more energy, not less — and how to build it into your life in ways that feel natural and sustainable.

Reflect & Reset

Take a moment to consider your afternoons.

- What does your usual slump look like?
- Which quick fixes do you rely on that don't really work?
- Which of the seven resets in this chapter feels most realistic for you to try tomorrow?

Choose just one. Experiment with it. Notice how it changes your afternoon.

Chapter 7: Moving for Energy, Not Exhaustion

When people think about exercise, they often imagine sweating through a punishing workout at the gym, running miles they don't enjoy, or following an intense programme designed to "burn calories" or "get results." For many of us, that image alone is enough to make us feel tired before we've even started.

But here's the truth: movement doesn't need to exhaust you to be effective. In fact, the best kind of movement for energy is often the opposite of what fitness culture sells. Instead of draining you, it should leave you feeling more alive, more focused, and more capable of tackling the rest of your day.

This chapter is about reframing the way you think about exercise. Movement is not a punishment for what you've eaten, and it's not a chore to be ticked off. It's a tool — one of the most reliable tools we have — for creating energy.

Why Movement Boosts Energy

On the surface, it seems strange. You'd think that using energy to move would leave you with less energy overall. But the human body doesn't work that way. Regular movement actually improves the systems that create energy in the first place.

Here's how:

- **Circulation**: Movement gets your blood pumping, delivering oxygen and nutrients to your muscles and brain.

- **Mitochondria**: These "powerhouses" of your cells multiply and function better when you move regularly, meaning your body produces energy more efficiently.

- **Hormones**: Movement stimulates endorphins, which lift mood and reduce stress. It also helps regulate cortisol, the stress hormone that can otherwise drain you.

- **Mental clarity**: Even a short walk can sharpen focus, refresh your thinking, and clear mental fog.

The key is consistency, not intensity. Small amounts of regular movement do far more for your energy than occasional bursts of all-out effort.

The Problem with Over-Exercising

Some people go to the other extreme, believing that more is always better. Long, gruelling workouts or daily high-intensity training can actually backfire, leaving you depleted, sore, and at greater risk of injury or burnout.

Exercise is a stress on the body — which can be good, in the right amount. But too much stress without enough recovery tips the energy equation in the wrong direction. Instead of building resilience, you end up draining your reserves.

If you've ever finished a workout feeling wiped out for hours afterwards, you know this firsthand. Exercise should lift you, not flatten you.

Finding the Energy "Sweet Spot"

So what's the right balance? Think of movement in three categories:

1. **Micro-movements** – The small actions that break up sitting: standing to stretch, walking to make a call, taking the stairs. These are short, but when repeated throughout the day, they add up significantly.

2. **Everyday activity** – Walking, gardening, playing with your children or dogs, housework. These are not "workouts," but they keep your body active and your energy steady.

3. **Intentional exercise** – More structured movement like running, cycling, swimming, strength training, or yoga. These build stamina, strength, and resilience.

The sweet spot is having a balance of all three, with a particular emphasis on micro-movements and everyday activity if your main goal is energy. You don't need long, punishing gym sessions. In fact, 20–30 minutes of moderate activity most days, combined with daily movement breaks, is more than enough to transform your energy.

Practical Resets with Movement

Here are some ways to bring more energising movement into your day:

- **Desk stretches**: Every hour, stand up and stretch your arms overhead, roll your shoulders, or bend gently side to side.

- **Walking meetings**: If possible, take a phone call or meeting while walking. Even pacing around your room helps.

- **10-minute walks**: A short walk after lunch or dinner helps stabilise blood sugar and refreshes your mind.

- **Bodyweight mini-routines**: Pick two or three simple moves (squats, push-ups, planks) and do them for five minutes. Enough to activate your muscles without draining you.

- **Active rest**: Instead of scrolling on your phone, do a short tidy-up, stretch, or go outside. These small swaps accumulate energy instead of depleting it.

The Role of Joyful Movement

One of the most overlooked aspects of exercise is enjoyment. Too often, movement is framed as punishment or obligation. But when you choose activities you enjoy, you're far more likely to stick with them — and they give you more emotional energy as well as physical.

Think about the activities that feel playful, freeing, or simply satisfying: dancing, hiking, yoga, cycling, swimming, or even just walking in nature. When you enjoy the process, movement stops being a task and becomes something you look forward to.

Personal Reflection: From Punishment to Fuel

There was a time when I thought exercise had to be all-or-nothing. I'd sign up for gym memberships or classes, throw myself into it for a few weeks, and then burn out.

The workouts left me drained, and eventually I gave up altogether.

What changed was reframing movement as fuel rather than punishment. I started with short walks, stretching, and simple bodyweight exercises at home. I stopped worrying about how many calories I was burning and focused on how I felt afterwards. Slowly, exercise shifted from being a chore to being one of my most reliable energy resets.

Why This Matters for Your Energy Reset

When you think of movement as a way to generate energy, not deplete it, everything changes. You stop dreading workouts and start seeing them as gifts to yourself. You stop pushing through exhaustion and start tuning in to what your body needs.

The most effective exercise routine is the one you can enjoy and sustain. Consistency is more powerful than intensity. And when your goal is energy, even the smallest actions make a noticeable difference.

Looking Ahead

In the next chapter, we'll move beyond the physical and explore another major energy drain: stress. Because even if you're eating well, moving regularly, and starting your mornings strong, unmanaged stress can pull the plug on your energy reserves faster than anything else.

Reflect & Reset

Take a few minutes to reflect:

- How do you currently think about exercise — as fuel, or as punishment?

- Do your current workouts leave you energised or exhausted?

- What small, enjoyable movement could you add into your day this week?

Remember: energy doesn't come from doing more. It comes from doing what sustains you.

Chapter 8: Stress Less, Recharge More

You can be doing everything "right" — eating balanced meals, moving regularly, getting decent sleep — and still feel tired. Why? Because stress can drain your energy faster than almost anything else.

Think of stress as an app running in the background of your phone. Even if you're not actively using it, it quietly consumes power. When your stress is constant, your body stays in a state of high alert, burning through resources and leaving you depleted.

This chapter is about recognising how stress affects your energy and learning small, realistic ways to manage it. Because while you can't eliminate stress completely, you can reduce its impact and recharge more effectively.

Why Stress Drains Energy

Stress is your body's natural survival mechanism. When you perceive a threat, your brain releases hormones like cortisol and adrenaline. These raise your heart rate, sharpen your senses, and prepare you to respond.

In the short term, this response is useful. But modern stressors — emails, deadlines, bills, family pressures — don't come and go quickly. They linger. Your body stays in alert mode long after the "threat" has passed. That's when stress becomes chronic.

Chronic stress drains energy in several ways:

- **Hormonal imbalance**: Elevated cortisol disrupts sleep and appetite.

- **Tension**: Muscles tighten, leaving you physically fatigued.

- **Mental load**: Worry consumes focus and concentration.

- **Emotional strain**: Irritability and anxiety erode emotional energy.

Over time, this constant drain leaves you feeling like you're running on empty, even if you're doing everything else "right."

The Stress-Energy Cycle

Stress and energy create a feedback loop. When you're stressed, you feel tired. When you're tired, you feel less able to cope, which makes stress feel worse. That cycle can become self-perpetuating unless you find a way to interrupt it.

The good news is, you don't need hours of meditation or a complete life overhaul to reduce stress. Small, intentional resets throughout the day can lower stress hormones, relax your body, and restore energy.

Reset 1: The Power of the Pause

One of the simplest ways to break the stress cycle is to pause — deliberately. Taking even 60 seconds to stop, breathe, and check in with yourself helps shift your body from "fight or flight" into "rest and digest."

Try this mini-reset:

- Sit comfortably.

- Inhale slowly through your nose for four counts.

- Exhale gently through your mouth for six counts.

- Repeat for one to two minutes.

This longer exhale signals safety to your nervous system, reducing cortisol and helping your body recharge.

Reset 2: Move Stress Out of Your Body

Stress isn't just in your head — it lives in your body too. That's why physical movement is one of the fastest ways to release it.

- Take a brisk five-minute walk.

- Stretch your shoulders, back, and neck where tension collects.

- Try shaking out your arms and legs to physically "shake off" stress.

Even a short burst of movement signals to your body that the stress response is complete, allowing you to return to calm.

Reset 3: Reframe the Thought

Much of stress comes not from the event itself but from how we think about it. If your self-talk is "I can't handle this," your body reacts with more tension. Shifting that narrative, even slightly, can reduce stress.

Instead of "I'll never get this done," try: "I'll do the most important thing first."
Instead of "I can't cope," try: "This is hard, but I've handled hard things before."

This isn't about ignoring reality — it's about choosing thoughts that calm your system instead of inflaming it.

Reset 4: Create Micro-Breaks

Many people wait until they're overwhelmed to take a break. By then, the stress response is already high. Building in short, regular breaks prevents stress from escalating.

Ideas for micro-breaks:

- Step outside for a few breaths of fresh air.

- Make a cup of tea and drink it slowly, without multitasking.

- Do a two-minute stretch at your desk.

- Listen to one favourite song.

These small pauses give your nervous system space to recover, keeping stress from draining your energy reserves.

Reset 5: Boundaries with Technology

Phones, emails, and notifications are among the biggest hidden stressors. The constant pings keep your nervous system on edge, preventing true rest. Setting boundaries helps you recharge.

- Turn off non-essential notifications.

- Check emails at set times instead of constantly.

- Avoid screens in the first and last 30 minutes of the day.

Protecting even small pockets of time from digital demands creates breathing space for your mind.

Reset 6: The Role of Connection

Stress feels heavier when carried alone. Talking to a friend, sharing your worries, or even just being with others who understand can lighten the load. Social connection releases oxytocin, a hormone that counteracts stress and restores calm.

Connection doesn't have to be deep or lengthy — even a short chat with a colleague or a text to a friend can help. The key is to remember you don't have to handle stress in isolation.

Personal Reflection: Stress in Daily Life

When I was balancing work, parenting, and the aftermath of a break-up, stress felt constant. Even when nothing was actively going wrong, my body was always braced, always tight. I'd collapse into bed exhausted but unable to sleep because my mind wouldn't switch off.

What helped wasn't one big solution, but a series of small resets. Pausing to breathe before picking my child up from school. A short walk with the dogs after stressful calls. Switching off emails after a certain time. None of these erased the stressors, but they stopped them from consuming all my energy.

Why Stress Management Is Essential for Energy

You can eat perfectly and sleep for eight hours, but if your stress is unrelieved, you'll still feel drained. Managing stress is not a luxury — it's an essential part of your energy equation.

Think of it this way: stress is like a slow leak in your battery. Unless you patch the leak, no amount of charging will keep you full. By using resets to manage stress, you keep more of the energy you already have.

Looking Ahead

In the next chapter, we'll shift focus to mindset. Because the way you think about your energy, your habits, and yourself has a profound effect on how energised you feel. By changing your mental patterns, you can create a lasting foundation for vitality.

Reflect & Reset

Take a moment to consider:

- What are your biggest daily stressors?

- How do they show up in your body — tension, headaches, racing thoughts?

- Which of the resets in this chapter could you try this week to release stress before it drains your energy?

Remember, stress isn't always in your control, but your response to it is. By choosing even one small reset, you shift your body back toward calm — and protect your energy.

Chapter 9: Your Energy Mindset

By now, you've learned how to start your mornings strong, fuel your body without the crash, beat the midday slump, move for energy, and manage stress. These practical steps make a huge difference. But there's one more piece of the puzzle that ties everything together: mindset.

The way you *think* about your energy influences your habits, your motivation, and even your biology. If you believe you're "always tired" or that low energy is just who you are, you'll unconsciously act in ways that reinforce that belief. On the other hand, if you believe your energy can improve — even by small amounts — you'll look for opportunities to recharge and make choices that support vitality.

This chapter is about shifting from a mindset of depletion to a mindset of energy.

The Stories We Tell Ourselves

Everyone carries an inner narrative about energy. You might hear yourself saying:

- "I'm just not a morning person."

- "I don't have the willpower to exercise."

- "I'll never have the energy other people seem to have."

These stories feel true because you've repeated them often. But in reality, they're habits of thought — not facts. And like any habit, they can be changed.

When you start telling yourself a different story — "I can wake up with more energy if I build the right habits" —

your actions shift. You try new strategies, notice small improvements, and gradually rewrite the pattern.

How Mindset Affects Energy

Mindset influences energy in several ways:

- **Focus**: If you believe you're always tired, your brain looks for evidence to confirm it. You notice every yawn, every dip, every foggy moment. But if you believe energy is possible, you notice small wins instead.

- **Motivation**: When you think "what's the point," you're less likely to try. When you think "this small reset helps," you're more willing to take action.

- **Stress response**: Negative thoughts amplify stress, which drains energy further. Positive, hopeful thoughts reduce stress, leaving more energy in the tank.

- **Resilience**: With the right mindset, setbacks become opportunities to reset rather than reasons to give up.

In short: mindset shapes behaviour, behaviour shapes results, and results reinforce mindset. By breaking into that loop, you can start building a more energised identity.

Reset 1: Notice Your Language

The first step is awareness. Pay attention to the way you talk about energy, both out loud and in your head. Do you often say, "I'm shattered," "I can't cope," or "I'm always exhausted"?

It's not about denying how you feel — it's about recognising that repeating those phrases makes them more ingrained. Try replacing them with gentler, more constructive statements:

- Instead of "I'm always tired," say "I'm learning how to restore my energy."

- Instead of "I can't do this," say "I'll take one small step."

Language matters. It sets the frame for how your brain interprets your experience.

Reset 2: Celebrate Small Wins

Many people think they'll feel energised only after a dramatic transformation. But waiting for big wins means you miss the small victories along the way.

Start celebrating the little shifts:

- You went to bed 30 minutes earlier.

- You chose water before coffee.

- You took a short walk instead of scrolling.

Each small win is proof that you're capable of change. Acknowledging them strengthens your belief that energy is possible — and builds momentum for more.

Reset 3: Reframe Setbacks

Setbacks are inevitable. You'll have days when you skip the walk, stay up too late, or give in to the vending machine. The old mindset says, "I've failed, so there's no point." The energy mindset says, "This is one moment — I can reset now."

Reframing setbacks stops you from spiralling and helps you get back on track quickly. It's the difference between one bad day and a bad month.

Reset 4: Visualise Your Energised Self

Take a moment to imagine yourself living with steady energy. Picture a typical day: how you wake up, how you move through work, how you interact with your family, how you feel in the evening.

Visualisation primes your brain to look for opportunities that align with that image. It's not about pretending — it's about rehearsing success so your mind and body are ready to create it.

Reset 5: Anchor Your Identity

One of the most powerful mindset shifts comes from changing how you see yourself. Instead of "I'm someone who is always tired," try anchoring to a new identity: "I'm someone who takes care of my energy."

When your actions flow from identity, they become easier to maintain. You don't have to force yourself to take breaks or drink water — it becomes natural because it's "what someone like me does."

Personal Reflection: Rewriting My Own Story

For a long time, my self-talk was negative. I'd tell friends, "I'm always exhausted," half-joking but half-resigned. I believed my tiredness was permanent — the inevitable result of working full-time, raising a child, and managing life's pressures.

The shift came slowly, when I started noticing the days I felt slightly better. Instead of brushing those off as flukes, I began seeing them as evidence that change was possible. That small mindset shift gave me motivation to keep experimenting with resets. Over time, my narrative changed from "I'm always exhausted" to "I know how to reset when I need to."

Why Mindset Completes the Energy Equation

You've learned throughout this book that energy is influenced by sleep, food, movement, and stress. But without the right mindset, it's hard to sustain progress. Mindset is what helps you keep going when you slip up, notice progress when it's small, and believe that change is worth the effort.

In other words, mindset turns actions into habits, and habits into a lifestyle.

Looking Ahead

In the final chapter, we'll bring everything together into a 30-day Energy Reset plan. This plan isn't about perfection — it's about building realistic, sustainable habits that fit into your life. Step by step, you'll see how small resets combine to create lasting energy.

Reflect & Reset

Take a moment to reflect:

- What stories do you currently tell yourself about your energy?

- How does that language affect the choices you make?

- What new, energising identity could you start to adopt?

Write down one phrase that reframes your mindset — something like "I'm someone who takes care of my energy." Keep it somewhere visible. Each time you see it, let it remind you that energy is not just physical — it's also mental.

Chapter 10: Your 30-Day Energy Reset Plan

You've reached the final chapter. By now, you've discovered why energy is so often drained, how the energy equation works, and the resets you can use to feel more alive — from better mornings to fuelling without the crash, beating the slump, moving for energy, reducing stress, and shifting your mindset.

But information alone isn't enough. What matters is putting it into action in a way that's realistic and sustainable. That's what this 30-Day Energy Reset is for: a practical roadmap that shows you how to build energising habits step by step, without overwhelm.

This is not a strict programme or a rigid challenge. It's flexible, adaptable, and designed to fit into real life. The aim is progress, not perfection. Each week builds on the last, gradually layering small resets until they become part of your everyday routine.

How the 30-Day Reset Works

- **Four weeks, four focus areas.** Each week has a theme drawn from the chapters of this book.

- **Small daily actions.** You'll add one or two resets at a time, keeping it simple.

- **Build, don't overhaul.** The goal is to strengthen your energy equation steadily, not all at once.

- **Reflect and reset.** At the end of each week, you'll pause, review, and adjust.

By the end of 30 days, you'll have a personalised toolkit of habits that support your energy long-term.

Week 1: Start Your Day Strong

Focus: Light, movement, hydration, and mindset.

Daily actions:

- Drink a glass of water first thing in the morning.
- Get at least five minutes of natural light (step outside, open curtains wide).
- Add two to five minutes of gentle movement (stretching, walking, yoga).
- Choose one mindset cue (e.g., "What's one thing I'm looking forward to today?").

Why it matters: This week is about flipping your body's natural "wake-up switches." You're teaching your system to start with energy rather than stress or autopilot.

End-of-week reflection:

- Which morning reset felt easiest?
- Which one made the biggest difference?
- What small adjustment will make it easier next week?

Week 2: Fuel Without the Crash

Focus: Balanced meals, hydration, and smart snacks.

Daily actions:

- Eat breakfast that includes protein (eggs, yoghurt, nuts, beans).

- At lunch, aim for a balance of protein, fibre, and healthy fats.

- Have one smart snack (fruit + protein, or wholegrain + fat).

- Drink water regularly — aim for 6–8 glasses.

Why it matters: This week you're stabilising your blood sugar, preventing the highs and lows that drain energy.

End-of-week reflection:

- Did you notice fewer crashes in the afternoon?

- Which snack or meal swap worked best for you?

- Are you drinking enough water, or do you need reminders?

Week 3: Beat the Slump and Move for Energy

Focus: Midday resets and everyday movement.

Daily actions:

- Take at least one five-minute movement break every 90–120 minutes.

- If you feel a slump, try one quick reset (walk, stretch, hydrate, breathe).

- Add one extra burst of everyday activity (walk, housework, gardening).

- Do one short, intentional exercise session (10–20 minutes) three times this week.

Why it matters: This week you're learning to recharge instead of push through. You're also reframing exercise as fuel, not punishment.

End-of-week reflection:

- Which midday reset worked best for you?

- Did short exercise sessions leave you energised or drained?

- How can you build more micro-movements into your day?

Week 4: Stress Less, Mindset More

Focus: Stress management and identity shifts.

Daily actions:

- Take one one-minute pause each day to breathe deeply.

- Create one micro-break during your workday (tea break, step outside, listen to music).

- Reframe one stressful thought with a calmer alternative.

- Write down one small win or energy success each day.

Why it matters: This week you're addressing the mental side of energy — reducing leaks from stress and building a mindset that supports lasting change.

End-of-week reflection:

- Which stress reset helped you most?

- What language do you use about your energy now?

- How has your overall energy shifted since Day 1?

Putting It All Together

After 30 days, you'll have tried resets for mornings, fuelling, movement, stress, and mindset. Some will feel natural, others less so. The goal is not to do them all perfectly — it's to notice which ones work best for you and keep those going.

Energy is deeply personal. Your ideal toolkit might be different from mine, or from anyone else's. That's why this reset isn't a "one size fits all plan." It's a framework you can adapt and revisit whenever you need to recharge.

Personal Reflection: The Power of Gradual Change

When I first tried to change my energy habits, I wanted results overnight. I tried cutting caffeine completely, overhauling my diet, and committing to ambitious workouts all at once. It lasted about a week before I crashed back into old patterns.

What worked, eventually, was slowing down. Choosing one or two resets at a time. Celebrating small wins. Forgiving myself when I slipped, and resetting again the next day.

That's the approach I've built into this 30-day plan. Because the truth is, lasting energy doesn't come from extremes — it comes from consistency. From choosing, again and again, to add just one more input into your energy equation.

Beyond 30 Days: Living the Energy Reset

The 30-Day Reset is a starting point, not an ending. Here are some ways to carry it forward:

- **Repeat it**: Each month, choose one focus area to strengthen again.

- **Adapt it**: If life changes, adjust the resets to fit your new rhythm.

- **Return to it**: When you feel drained, revisit the plan as a toolkit to recharge.

Energy isn't something you achieve once. It's something you cultivate daily. The good news is, every small action counts.

Reflect & Reset

As you finish this book, pause to reflect:

- What have you learned about your own energy over the last 30 days?

- Which resets feel most natural to you?

- How do you want to carry this forward into the months ahead?

Write down your personal "Energy Toolkit" — a short list of the three to five resets that make the biggest difference for you. Keep it somewhere you'll see it often.

Remember: you don't have to overhaul your life to feel better. You just need to keep choosing small, steady resets. Over time, those choices add up to more energy, more clarity, and more life.

Conclusion: More Energy, More Life

You've reached the end of *The Energy Reset*. Over these chapters, we've explored why energy so often feels out of reach and, more importantly, how you can begin to restore it with small, realistic resets.

You've learned that energy isn't just about willpower, or about pushing through. It's about balance. It's about noticing the inputs that fuel you — sleep, food, movement, rest, mindset, connection — and reducing the outputs that drain you — stress, overwork, poor habits, negative self-talk.

Most of all, you've learned that change doesn't have to be dramatic to be powerful. In fact, the most lasting changes are usually the smallest.

The Journey You've Taken

Let's pause and recap the journey you've just completed:

- In the early chapters, you uncovered why you're always tired, how the energy equation works, and how mornings can act as a reset button for the entire day.

- You learned how to fuel your body without the crash, stabilising your energy with simple food and hydration choices.

- You discovered how to beat the midday slump with quick resets that take minutes but can save hours of sluggishness.

- You reframed movement as something that gives energy, not something that depletes it.

- You recognised the hidden toll of stress and practised ways to calm your system and recharge.

- And finally, you shifted your mindset — learning to celebrate small wins, reframe setbacks, and anchor your identity as someone who takes care of their energy.

Then, through the 30-Day Reset plan, you brought it all together into a practical roadmap. Step by step, you built a personal toolkit that you can return to whenever life leaves you feeling drained.

Where You Go From Here

The real question now is: what comes next?

The answer is not perfection. You won't follow every reset every day. You'll have weeks where you slip back into old patterns, or days when energy feels low no matter what you do. That's normal.

The goal isn't to never get tired. It's to know how to reset when you do.

That's the real gift of this book. It's not a promise of boundless energy forever. It's the knowledge that you can take back control of your energy, one small choice at a time.

When you start your morning with a glass of water, step outside for a few minutes of daylight, stretch between meetings, or reframe a stressful thought, you are proving something powerful: that you can influence your energy. That you are not helpless. That even on your busiest or hardest days, you can choose to reset.

My Final Reflection

When I began writing this book, I thought about the years when I was constantly running on empty. Balancing full-time work, raising a child, looking after two dogs, and navigating the emotional strain of a break-up — I know what it's like to feel depleted.

Back then, I believed tiredness was inevitable, that exhaustion was just part of being an adult. What I've learned since is that while life will always bring demands, we don't have to accept depletion as our normal state.

Energy is something we can build, protect, and renew. Not through extremes, but through steady, realistic habits that fit our lives.

And if I can do it in the middle of life's chaos, so can you.

A Gentle Call to Action

Before you close this book, I'd like to invite you to do two things:

1. **Keep using your toolkit.**
   Look back over your notes, highlights, and reflections. Choose the three to five resets that make the biggest difference for you. Make them your non-negotiables. These will be your anchors, the habits you return to whenever life gets busy or overwhelming.

2. **Share your experience.**
   If you've found this book helpful, I'd love for you to leave a short review. Your words don't just support me as an author — they help other tired, busy people discover that there's a way forward. Reviews make a real difference, and your perspective may be exactly what someone else needs to see to take the first step.

More Energy, More Life

Ultimately, this book has never been about chasing perfection or squeezing more productivity out of your day. It's about something much deeper: reclaiming the energy you need to live fully.

Because when you have energy, everything changes. You show up differently for your family, your work, and yourself. You notice more, enjoy more, and feel more capable. You move from surviving to thriving.

So take these resets with you. Use them as often as you need. And remember — you don't need to do everything at once. One glass of water. One walk. One pause to breathe.

That's how energy is built: small step by small step, reset by reset.

Here's to more energy. Here's to more clarity. Here's to more life.

Bonus Resources: Your Energy Toolkit

This section pulls together the key resets from the book into simple, practical tools you can use anytime. Keep this as your quick reference guide — whether you need a reminder in the middle of a busy day, or a reset plan when your energy dips.

Daily Energy Checklist

Use this simple list to anchor your energy habits each day:

Morning

- Drink a glass of water before coffee.

- Get at least five minutes of natural light.

- Do two to five minutes of gentle movement.

- Ask: *"What's one thing I'm looking forward to today?"*

Throughout the Day

- Eat balanced meals (protein + fibre + healthy fats).

- Take a five-minute break every 90–120 minutes.

- Move regularly (walk, stretch, stairs, tidy-up tasks).

- Drink water consistently.

Evening

- Set a screen-free wind-down routine.

- Write down one small win or moment of gratitude.

- Aim for a consistent bedtime.

Quick Resets for When Energy Dips

If you hit a slump, choose one of these fast-acting resets:

- **Move:** Stand, stretch, or walk for 3–5 minutes.

- **Hydrate:** Drink a glass of water or herbal tea.

- **Breathe:** Inhale for 4 counts, exhale for 6. Repeat for 2 minutes.

- **Refocus:** Look out of a window at the horizon or sky.

- **Snack smart:** Pair fruit with protein or healthy fat (apple + nuts, crackers + hummus).

- **Reframe:** Replace "I can't cope" with "I'll do one thing now."

Your Energy Emergency Plan

For days when you feel completely drained, use this simple three-step plan:

1. **Pause and reset your breath.** Two minutes of slow, deep breathing.

2. **Do one physical reset.** Stretch, walk, or drink water.

3. **Do one mental reset.** Write down the *next smallest task* and focus only on that.

You may not feel perfect afterwards, but you'll feel better than before — and that's progress.

Your Personal Top 5 Resets

Not every reset in this book will be right for you. The goal is to build your own toolkit of the ones that make the biggest difference. Take a moment now to write down your personal "Top 5":

1. ——————————————————————————

2. ——————————————————————————

3. ——————————————————————————

4. ——————————————————————————

5. ——————————————————————————

Keep this list somewhere visible — on your fridge, by your desk, or saved in your phone. Whenever your energy dips, return to it.

Final Note

Energy is not about doing more — it's about doing what sustains you. Use these resets as often as you need and remember: every small step counts.

About the Author

Amelia Walsh is the creator of the *Everyday Reset* series, a collection of practical, uplifting guides designed to help people make small, sustainable changes that add up to big results. Her books focus on simple, science-backed habits that fit into busy lives — from gratitude and decluttering, to walking, connection, and energy.

Amelia writes not from the perspective of perfection, but from real life. As a full-time working parent balancing the demands of family, work, and two energetic dogs, she knows what it feels like to be stretched thin. She also knows the power of resetting — of finding small, practical steps that restore balance and create space for more joy.

Her writing is warm, accessible, and deeply encouraging. Each book is designed as a toolkit, offering realistic resets that readers can apply straight away, even on the busiest of days.

When she's not writing, Amelia can often be found outdoors walking, reading in cosy corners, or enjoying time with her daughter.

You can explore more of her books in the *Everyday Reset* series, including *The Gratitude Reset*, *The Decluttering Reset*, *The Walking Reset*, and *The Connection Reset*.

Printed in Dunstable, United Kingdom